篮球技术统计员手册

中国篮球协会　审定

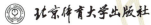

北京体育大学出版社

FOREWORD

Throughout the FIBA Statisticians' Manual, all references made to a player, coach, official etc. in the male gender also apply to the female gender. It must be understood that this is done for practical reasons only.

The statisticians' responsibility is to record what has happened on the court. The manual provides hard and fast guidelines to help the statistician avoid guessing. For any situation not covered by this manual, the statistician must use his best judgement to record the play.

In example situations, team A refers to the offensive team, team B to the defensive team. Official Interpretations appear within every section. A thorough understanding of the Official Basketball Rules is necessary in order to perform the statisticians' role.

前言

- 整本《篮球技术统计员手册》中所有提到的运动员、教练员、技术官员等都是男性，同样也适用于女性。必须理解到，这样写只是为了实用的缘故。

- 技术统计员的职责是记录赛场上发生的一切。本手册将提供坚实而快捷的指导方针，避免技术统计员根据猜测作出决定。技术统计员必须就手册中未涵盖的比赛情况作出最佳判断并做记录。

- 在比赛情况举例中，A队是进攻队，B队是防守队。在手册的每一章节中都会出现规则解释。通晓篮球规则是能够胜任技术统计员的必要条件。

（本手册王潇凌参与了翻译工作，安一媚参与了编校组织工作。）

TABLE OF CONTENTS

目录

第1章
ONE - FIELD GOALS
投篮得分

ONE- FIELD GOALS

A field goal attempt (FGA) is charged to a player any time he shoots, throws or tips a live ball at his opponent's basket in an attempt to score a goal.

A field goal made (FGM) is charged to a player any time a FGA taken by him results in a goal being scored, or being awarded because of illegal interference with the ball (goal tending) by a defensive player.

- A FGA can occur from anywhere on the court, regardless of the shooting motion.
- A FGA at the end of a period counts as a FGA, if the ball was released before the buzzer.
- A player fouled in the act of shooting is not charged with a FGA unless the field goal is made.
- A field goal attempt (FGA) is not charged to the shooter if the shot is nullified because of illegal interference with the ball (goal tending) by an offensive player.
- A FGA is not charged if the player is shooting the ball when a team-mate commits a violation or foul, just prior to the ball being released. When this foul or violation is committed after the ball has been released, a FGA is charged.
- A tip (also called put-back) by an offensive player counts as a FGA (and an offensive rebound) if the player's tip was under control. If the tip is successful, FGA and FGM are credited regardless of control.
- In the case of a shot being blocked before the ball is released, a FGA is recorded.

When a field goal is the result of a defensive player accidentally scoring in his team's own basket, the score will be charged to the court captain of the opposition team. The court captain, will be charged with both a FGA and a FGM. In case the own goal occurred during a rebound situation after a missed

第1章　投篮得分

一次试投（FGA）应被登记给一名队员，当他将活球向对方的球篮投、掷、拍以尝试一次得分时。

一次投中（FGM）应被登记给一名队员，当他进行一次试投，结果球中篮得分或者因防守队员发生干扰得分（干涉得分）致使得分有效。

- 一次试投可以发生在赛场上的任何地点，无论以何种投篮动作完成。
- 一次临近某节比赛结束时的试投只要球在蜂鸣器响之前离手，就应被登记。
- 一名在做投篮动作的队员被犯规时的试投不应被登记，除非投中。
- 如果因为一名进攻队员发生了干扰得分（干涉得分）而导致投篮无效，该试投就不应被登记给投篮队员。
- 如果在一名队员投篮球离手之前，他的同队队员发生了一起违例或者犯规，该试投就不应被登记；然而如果这起犯规或者违例发生在球离手之后，则该试投应被登记。
- 一名进攻队员向对方球篮的拍击球（也被称作补篮）应被登记为一次试投（同时还应登记一次进攻篮板球），前提是该拍击动作是队员可控制的。如果一次拍击球中篮，那么不管动作是否是可控制的，试投和投中均应被登记。
- 在一次投篮的球离手前被封盖的情况下，一次试投应被登记。

防守队员意外地使球进入本方球篮的得分应被登记给对方球队的场上队长。该场上队长将同时被登记一次试投和一次投中。如果在一次进攻队不成功的试投后抢篮板球时发生了上述情况，进攻队还应被登记一次球

FGA of the offensive team, his team will be credited with an offensive team rebound. In situations other than rebound ones, if the same team was in possession before scoring an own basket, a turnover needs to be given to the player scoring the own basket.

Fast-break Points

Are points scored quickly (max. 8 seconds) and at full speed by a team before their opponent has had time to set their half-court defence following a change in possession. The change of possession may be due to a turnover, defensive rebound or a FGM and are all counted as fast-break points. The points can come from a FGM and / or FTM(s) - including those resulting from any foul committed during a fast-break situation. Fast-break points are also possible after an offensive rebound (for example after a missed layup during a fast-break), assuming that at the moment the team scored after the offensive rebound the defence was still not set.

Examples

1. A5 shoots but fouls B5 (a) before the ball is in flight or (b) after the ball is in flight and field goal is not made or (c) after the ball is in flight and field goal is made.

(a) No FGA A5; turnover (offensive foul) A5; personal foul A5; foul drawn B5.
(b) FGA A5; personal foul A5, defensive team rebound Team B; foul drawn B5.
(c) FGA/FGM A5; personal foul A5; foul drawn B5.

If in doubt about whether the foul occurred before or after the ball was in flight, the actions of the officials will indicate the correct ruling. If the foul occurred before the ball was in flight, it will be signalled as a "team control foul". If the foul occurred after the ball was in flight, the official will not indicate team control.

2. A2 shoots a FGA, and in the fight for the rebound B5 accidentally tips the ball into his own basket.

FGA A2; Offensive team rebound Team A; FGA/FGM is charged to the court captain of the offensive team (Team A).

3. With one second left in the third period, B4 captures a defensive rebound in his own half, then turns and tosses the ball at the opponents' basket with the ball being released (a) before the buzzer (b) after the buzzer.

队篮板球。而在非抢篮板球的情况下，如果使球进入本方球篮的球队和先前拥有球权的球队是同一队的话，应登记使球进入本方球篮的队员一次失误。

快攻得分

因对方失误、抢得防守篮板球、对方投中等情况而发生球权转换后，某队在对方尚未建立半场防守位置时以全速（8秒内）完成的任何得分，均记作快攻得分。快攻得分包括投中和／或罚球得分，包括在快攻中因发生犯规而导致的罚球。快攻得分还可能发生在抢得一次进攻篮板球后（比如在快攻中上篮未中篮后），前提是在抢得进攻篮板球后得分时，对方依然没有回到防守位置。

举例

1. A5 投篮，但：（a）在球离手前对 B5 犯规，或（b）当球已在空中飞行时对 B5 犯规，球未中篮，或（c）当球已在空中飞行时对 B5 犯规，球中篮。

（a）不登记试投；A5 失误（进攻犯规）；A5 侵人犯规；B5 被侵犯。

（b）A5 试投；A5 侵人犯规；B 队防守球队篮板球；B5 被侵犯。

（c）A5 试投和投中；A5 侵人犯规；B5 被侵犯。

如果对于犯规发生在球离手之前还是之后存在疑问，裁判员的手势将给出正确的判定。如果球离手前发生犯规，那么手势是"控制球队犯规"；如果球离手后发生犯规，裁判员不会做控制球队犯规的手势。

2. A2 进行试投，球仍在空中时，B5 为了争抢篮板球而意外地将球拍入了本方球篮。

A2 试投；A 队进攻球队篮板球；登记进攻球队（A 队）场上队长一次试投和投中。

3. 第 3 节还剩 1 秒时，B4 在本方球篮的半场抢得防守篮板球后，随即转身将球掷向对方球篮，球离手发生在（a）蜂鸣器响之前；（b）蜂鸣器响之后。

(a)FGA B4; if the basket is made also charge him with a FGM.
(b)No action is recorded.

4. A1 shoots a FGA and the ball lodges on the basket support.

FGA A1. A team rebound is charged to the team gaining possession of the ball according to the alternating possession arrow.

5. Team B is in the penalty for the current period. A1 is driving to the basket and is fouled by B5 (a) before the shot; (b) in the act of shooting; (c) after the ball has been released. In all situations he misses the shot and two free-throws are awarded to him.

(a)Personal Foul B5; Foul Drawn A1. No FGA is credited.
(b)Shooting Foul B5; Foul Drawn A1. No FGA is credited.
(c)FGA A1; Offensive team rebound Team A; Personal Foul B5; Foul Drawn A1.

6. A3 is blocked by B2 during a jump shot before the ball is released. He lands with the ball in his hands and is called for a travel violation.

FGA A3; Blocked shot B2; Offensive rebound A3; Turnover (travelling) A3.

7. A1's pass is intercepted by B1. B1 throws a long pass to B2. B2 misses the layup. After taking the rebound, B2 passes the ball to B3 who makes a three-point shot. At the time of the shot the defense was still not set.

Turnover A1, Steal B1, FGA B2, Offensive Rebound B2, 3FGA and 3FGM B3, Assist B2. The 3FGM counts as Points off turnovers, Second Chance Points and Fast-break Points.

8. A1 misses a FGA and B1 retrieves the rebound. Immediately after taking the rebound, B1 is fouled by A3 and is awarded two FT's because of team fouls. He makes one of two FT's.

FGA A1, Defensive Rebound B1, Personal Foul A3, Foul Drawn B1, two times FTA and FTM B1 (NOT recorded as fast-break points).

9. A1 misses a FGA and B1 retrieves the rebound. After an outlet pass to B2, B2 is initiating a fast-break and is fouled by A2 to stop the fast-break. B2 is awarded two FT's because of team fouls and makes both.

FGA A1, Defensive Rebound B1, Personal Foul A2, Foul Drawn B2, two times FTA and FTM B2 (count as fast-break points).

（a）B4 试投；如球中篮，登记他一次投中。

（b）不做登记。

4. A1 进行试投，球停留在球篮支架上。

A1 试投；登记一次球队篮板球给根据交替拥有箭头获得球权的球队。

5. B 队在该节处于全队犯规处罚状态。A1 持球突破时被 B5 犯规（a）在投篮之前；（b）在做投篮动作时；（c）在球离手之后。在所有情况下，球均未中篮，并且他被判给 2 次罚球。

（a）B5 侵人犯规；A1 被侵犯。不登记试投。

（b）B5 对投篮队员犯规；A1 被侵犯。不登记试投。

（c）A1 试投；A 队进攻球队篮板球；B5 侵人犯规；A1 被侵犯。

6. A3 跳投，在球离手前被 B2 封盖。他持球落地，并被宣判带球走违例。

A3 试投；B2 封盖；A3 进攻篮板球；A3 失误（带球走）。

7. A1 的传球被 B1 截断，B1 长传给 B2，B2 上篮未中篮。B2 获得篮板球并将球传给 B3，随后 B3 的 3 分投篮球中篮。该投篮发生时，A 队仍未回到防守位置。

A1 失误；B1 抢断；B2 试投；B2 进攻篮板球；B3 的 3 分试投和 3 分投中；B2 助攻。该 3 分投中应记作对方失误后得分、二次进攻得分和快攻得分。

8. A1 试投未中篮，B1 抢得篮板球。在 B1 获得篮板球后，A3 立即对他犯规，因全队犯规的原因，B1 被判给 2 次罚球。他 2 次罚球命中 1 分。

A1 试投；B1 防守篮板球；A3 侵人犯规；B1 被侵犯；B1 的 2 次罚球尝试和 1 次罚球得分（不记作快攻得分）。

9. A1 试投未中篮，B1 抢得篮板球后将球传给 B2，B2 发动快攻，A2 为阻止快攻对 B2 犯规。因全队犯规次数已满，B2 被判给 2 次罚球。他 2 次罚球均中篮。

A1 试投；B1 防守篮板球；A2 侵人犯规；B2 被侵犯；B2 的 2 次罚球尝试和罚球得分（记作快攻得分）。

10. A1's pass is intercepted by B2. B2 goes coast to coast, but misses the layup and rebounds his own shot. Afterwards Team B sets up a set play. Later during the same possession, A1 knocks the ball loose from B3, the ball goes out of bounds and is awarded to Team B for the throw in. Team B takes a timeout. With the shot clock expiring, B2 hits a difficult three-point shot from 10 metres.

Turnover (bad pass) A1, Steal B2, FGA B2, Offensive Rebound B2, Timeout Team B, 3FGA and 3FGM B2 (recorded as second chance points and points off turnovers) .

10. A1 传球被 B2 截断。B2 从后场运球至前场上篮未中篮，但抢得篮板球。然后，B 队展开阵地进攻。在同一攻防回合中，A1 将 B3 手中的球拍击出界，B 队获得掷球入界。B 队被准予一次暂停。随后在进攻时间即将结束时，B2 从 10 米外投入了一记高难度的 3 分球。

A1 失误（传球失误）；B2 抢断；B2 试投；B2 进攻篮板球；B 队暂停；B2 的 3 分试投和 3 分投中（记作二次进攻得分和对方失误后得分）。

第2章

TWO - FREE - THROWS

罚球

TWO -FREE-THROWS

A free-throw attempt (FTA) is charged to a player when that player shoots a free-throw, unless there is a violation by a defensive player and the shot misses. That is, a player should not be charged for a FTA that is influenced by the illegal actions of an opponent, unless the shot results in a free-throw made (FTM).

A FTM is charged to a player any time a free-throw attempt by that player results in a score of one point being awarded.

If there is a violation during the free-throws, the statistician should very clearly observe what the officials are awarding, who the violation was called on and what the result of the call is. The following statistics apply:

- When a player on the defensive team commits a violation
    - If the free-throw is successful, the score will count despite the defensive violation, so charge the free-throw shooter with a FTA and a FTM.
    - If the free-throw misses, do not charge the free-throw shooter with a FTA because they will be given a substitute free-throw. Ignore the missed free-throw and charge a FTA (and a FTM if successful) for the substitute free-throw.
- When the shooter commits a violation

    - If the free-throw is successful, it will be cancelled.
    - A FTA is charged to the shooter.
    - If the free-throw was the last of a series, the defensive team will be awarded possession out-of-bounds. Charge the defensive team with a team rebound.
- When a team-mate of the shooter commits a violation
    - The officials will not cancel a successful free-throw when an offensive player violates, so charge a FTA and a FTM to the free-throw shooter.

第 2 章　罚球

一次罚球尝试（FTA）应被登记给一名执行罚球的队员，除非一名防守队员发生了违例且球未中篮。即当对手的非法动作影响到罚球队员时，该罚球队员不应被登记一次罚球尝试，除非该罚球得分（FTM）。

每当一名队员的一次罚球尝试结果是得 1 分时，一次罚球得分就应被登记给这名队员。

如果在罚球期间出现违例，技术统计员应非常仔细地观察裁判员是否判给得分、宣判谁违例，以及宣判的结果是什么。数据应按下述方法登记：

- 当一名防守队员发生违例：
  - 如果罚球中篮，应计得分，忽略防守队员违例，登记罚球队员一次罚球尝试和一次罚球得分。
  - 如果罚球未中篮，不登记罚球队员的罚球尝试，因为他将被重新判给一次罚球。忽略未中篮的罚球，并为这次重新判给的罚球登记一次罚球尝试（如罚球中篮，同时登记罚球得分）。
- 当罚球队员发生违例：
  - 如果罚球中篮，应取消得分。
  - 登记罚球队员一次罚球尝试。
  - 如果这是单一罚球单元中的最后一次罚球，防守队将被判给掷球入界的球权。登记防守队一次球队篮板球。
- 当罚球队员的同队队员发生违例：
  - 当一名进攻队员在罚球期间发生违例且罚球中篮时，裁判员不会取消得分，而是登记罚球队员一次罚球尝试和一次罚球得分。

- o If the free-throw misses, the free-throw shooter is still charged with a FTA. If the free-throw was the last of a series, the defensive team will be awarded possession out-of-bounds. Charge the defensive team with a team rebound.

In all of the above situations, NO turnovers have occurred.

If a wrong player is attempting a free-throw, the official will cancel the FTM's and/or FTA's as a result of the error.

If a technical foul has resulted in free-throws being taken immediately before the start of a period, the FTA (and FTM if successful) shall be charged in the new period.

In all such "special" situations it is important that the statisticians follow the decisions of the referees and communicate with the table officials where necessary.

Examples

1. A1 shoots a free-throw and during the shot, B3 commits a free-throw violation. (a) The free-throw is made or (b) the free-throw misses.

(a) FTA and FTM A1. (b) Do not charge A1 with a FTA – a substitute free-throw will be awarded.

2. A5 shoots the last free-throw in a series and during the shot, A4 commits a violation. (a) The free-throw is made or (b) the free-throw misses.

(a) FTA and FTM A5. (b) FTA A5, Defensive Rebound Team B. No Turnover is charged.

○ 如果罚球未中篮，仍应登记罚球队员一次罚球尝试。如果这是单一罚球单元中的最后一次罚球，防守队将被判给掷球入界的球权。登记防守队一次球队篮板球。

在上述所有情况下均没有发生失误。

如果一名错误的队员尝试了罚球，作为可纠正失误的结果，裁判员会取消罚球得分和／或罚球尝试。

如果在一节开始前执行技术犯规带来的罚球，罚球尝试（如罚球中篮，同时登记罚球得分）应被登记在新的一节中。

在所有这类"特殊"情况下，技术统计员遵从裁判员的决定，并在必要时与记录台人员沟通，就显得格外重要。

举例

1. A1 执行一次罚球，在投篮期间，B3 发生违例。（a）罚球中篮，或（b）罚球未中篮。

（a）A1 罚球尝试和罚球得分；（b）不登记 A1 的罚球尝试，他将被重新判给一次罚球。

2. A5 执行单一罚球单元中的最后一次罚球，在投篮期间，A4 发生违例。（a）罚球中篮，或（b）罚球未中篮。

（a）A5 罚球尝试和罚球得分；（b）A5 罚球尝试，B队防守球队篮板球。不登记失误。

第 3 章
THREE - REBOUNDS
篮板球

THREE-REBOUNDS

Apart from the exceptions listed below, any missed FGA or last FTA is followed by a rebound. A rebound is the controlled recovery of a live ball by a player or a team being entitled to the ball for a throw-in after a missed FGA or last FTA.

Rebounds are divided into Offensive and Defensive. Offensive rebounds are charged when possession is retained by the same team who missed the FTA or FGA, while defensive rebounds are charged when possession is gained by the team who did not attempt to score.

The recovery may be accomplished by:
- Being first to gain control of the ball, even if the ball has touched several hands, bounced or rolled along the floor.
- Tipping the ball in a controlled attempt to score a goal.
- Tipping or deflecting the ball in a controlled manner to a team-mate.
- Retrieving a rebound simultaneously with an opposing player and having their team be awarded the ball as a result of the alternating possession.

A team rebound is charged to the team entitled to possession of the ball when:

- The ball goes out of bounds after a missed FGA or FTA and before any player gains control of the ball.
- A foul occurs after a missed FGA or FTA and before any player gains control of the ball.
- After a missed FTA or FGA two or more players from the same team are involved in a held-ball.
- The ball lodges between the ring and the backboard or on the basket support.
- An own basket occurs during a rebound situation (a defensive player tipping the ball accidentally in his own basket).

第3章 篮板球

除下文中列出的特例之外，在任何试投或最后一次罚球尝试未中篮后，都会出现一次篮板球。当一次试投或最后一次罚球尝试未中篮后，某队队员恢复控制活球或者某队获得掷球入界的球权，是一次篮板球。

篮板球被分为进攻篮板球和防守篮板球。当球权被试投或最后一次罚球尝试未中篮的球队重新获得，应登记为进攻篮板球；当球权被试投或最后一次罚球未中篮队的对方队获得，应登记为防守篮板球。

可通过以下形式恢复控制球（篮板球）：

- 成为第一名控制球的队员，即使球已经接触了多名队员的手、从地面弹起或者在地面滚动。
- 通过可控制的拍击球以尝试得分。
- 以可控制的方式将球拍击或拦截给同队队员。
- 和对方队员同时争抢篮板球，然后本方球队被判给交替拥有球权。

一次球队篮板球登记给获得球权的队，当：

- 一次试投或罚球尝试未中篮后，在任何队员获得控制球前球出界。
- 一次试投或罚球尝试未中篮后，在任何队员获得控制球前发生一起犯规。
- 一次试投或罚球尝试未中篮后，有两名或多于两名同队队员参与了一次争球情况。
- 球停留在篮圈和篮板之间或停留在球篮支架上。
- 争抢篮板球期间，球进入本方球篮（一名防守队员意外地将球拍入本方球篮）。

There are no rebounds charged:

- After any missed FTA where the ball will not be live.
- At the end of a period when the buzzer sounds after a missed FGA or FTA and before a team gains possession.
- After a missed FGA where the ball does not touch the ring, the twenty-four second device sounds and the officials blow their whistle to signal a twenty-four second violation before a player has a controlled recovery of the ball.

In situations in which a player rebound is followed immediately by a turnover by that same player (for example gaining control while being in the air and landing out of bounds), a team rebound can be given to the other team instead.

Examples

1. A missed shot is retrieved simultaneously by A5 and B4.

Rebound A5 or B4, depending on the alternating possession arrow.

2. After a missed shot by A3, A5 jumps and catches the ball, but falls and loses control. The shot clock is reset to 14. After A5 loses control, the ball is retrieved by B4.

Defensive Rebound B4. Note: even if this results in a contradiction between the decision of the referees (resetting the shot clock to 14 sec means they assumed A5 had control of the ball) and the statistics (awards the rebound to the player who finally assumed control, B4), this is the correct decision.

3. After a missed shot, B4 catches the ball at almost the same time as A5 fouls him.

The statistician must decide if B4 had control of the ball for a split-second before being fouled. If so, charge the rebound to B4. Otherwise, Team B is charged with a defensive team rebound.

4. A4 jumps and attempts a shot that is blocked by B5 without the ball leaving A4's hands. A4 lands with the ball and is called for a travelling violation.

FGA A4, Block B5, Offensive Rebound A4, Turnover A4 (Violation).

5. After a missed shot B2, B4 and A4 contest the rebound, getting both hands on the ball in a held-ball situation. (a) Team A are entitled to the alternating possession or (b) Team B are entitled to the alternating possession.

以下情况不登记篮板球：

- 在任何试投未中篮后，球不再是活球时。
- 在临近一节比赛结束时，一次试投或罚球尝试未中篮后，某队获得控制球前，蜂鸣器响起。
- 一次试投未中篮且未接触篮圈后，队员获得控制球前，进攻计时钟响起且裁判员鸣哨示意进攻时间违例。

在一名队员获得篮板球但随后该队员立即发生失误的情况下（如一名队员腾空控制篮板球后落到界线外），应登记对方队一次球队篮板球。

举例

1. 投篮未中篮后，A5 和 B4 同时争抢到了篮板球。

根据交替拥有的箭头指向，登记 A5 或 B4 篮板球。

2. A3 投篮未中篮后，A5 跳起后抓住球但在落地时摔倒并失去控制球。进攻计时钟被复位到 14 秒。A5 失去控制球后，B4 获得了控制球。

B4 防守篮板球。注意：即使裁判员的判定（将进攻计时钟复位至 14 秒意味着他们已假定 A5 获得了控制球）与数据统计（将篮板球登记给最终获得控制球的队员 B4）存在不一致，这也是正确的决定。

3. 投篮未中篮后，B4 抓住了球，几乎同时，A5 对他犯规。

技术统计员必须确定 B4 在被犯规前的一刻是否已经控制了球。如果是，登记 B4 篮板球；反之，则登记 B 队一次防守球队篮板球。

4. A4 跳起并尝试投篮时被 B5 封盖，但球没有离开 A4 的手。A4 落地，被宣判一起带球走违例。

A4 试投；B5 封盖；A4 进攻篮板球；A4 失误（违例）。

5. 投篮未中篮后，B2、B4 和 A4 争抢篮板球并都将手置于球上而形成了争球。（a）A 队获得交替拥有的球权，或（b）B 队获得交替拥有的球权。

(a) Off. Rebound A4.

(b) Def. Rebound Team B.

6. A3 misses a FGA and as players are fighting for the rebound (a) A4 is called for an over the back foul on B2 (b) B1 is called for a holding foul on A1 (c) B4 tips the ball out of bounds.

(a) Def. Rebound Team B.

(b) Off. Rebound Team A.

(c) Off. Rebound Team A.

7. A1 misses a FGA shortly before the twenty-four second device sounds, and the ball does not touch the ring (a) B2 catches the ball immediately before the device sounds (b) A2 catches the ball before the device sounds (c) A2 catches the ball after the device sounds.

All situations: FGA A1. (a) Def. Rebound B2. (b) Off. Rebound A2; Team Turnover (24 seconds) Team A. (c) Team Turnover (24 seconds) Team A. No rebound is charged as the ball is dead.

8. A2 misses the first of two free-throws.

There is no rebound as A2 is entitled to a second free-throw and the ball is dead.

9. A2 misses a FGA, and before any player retrieves the rebound, the period ends.

FGA A2. Do not charge any rebound as the ball is dead.

10. A3 misses a FGA and misses the rim; The ball hits the floor and A5 picks up the loose ball.

FGA A3, Off. Rebound A5.

11. A1 misses a FGA. A4 is fighting for the rebound with several other players. He tips the ball backwards out of the paint where it is picked up by A3.

FGA A1; Off. Rebound A3.

12. A1 misses a FGA. A4 is fighting with several other players for the rebound and is able to tip the ball in a controlled manner to A5 who makes immediately a 3FGM.

FGA A1; Off. Rebound A4; 3FGA and 3FGM A5; Assist A4.

13. A4 misses a FGA. A5 is jumping for the rebound, gains control but lands out of bounds.

FGA A4; Def. Rebound Team B.

（a）A4 进攻篮板球。

（b）B 队防守球队篮板球。

6. A3 试投未中篮，场上队员争抢篮板球时，（a）A4 被判从背后对 B2 犯规；（b）B1 被判对 A1 发生拉人犯规；（c）B4 将球拍出界。

（a）B 队防守球队篮板球。

（b）A 队进攻球队篮板球。

（c）A 队进攻球队篮板球。

7. A1 试投未中篮后不久，进攻计时钟响起，球未接触篮圈，（a）B2 在进攻计时钟响之前抓住了球；（b）A2 在进攻计时钟响之前抓住了球；（c）A2 在进攻计时钟响之后抓住了球。

在所有情况下：A1 试投。（a）B2 防守篮板球；（b）A2 进攻篮板球；A 队球队失误（24 秒）；（c）A 队球队失误（24 秒）。不登记篮板球，因为球已成死球。

8. A2 执行二次罚球，第一次罚球未中篮。

因为 A2 还有第二次罚球，所以不产生篮板球，且球已成死球。

9. A2 试投未中篮，在任何队员获得控制球前，该节结束了。

A2 试投。因球成死球，不登记篮板球。

10. A3 试投未中篮，球未接触球篮。球击地弹起后被 A5 控制。

A3 试投；A5 进攻篮板球。

11. A1 试投未中篮，A4 同其他几名队员争抢篮板球。他将球向后拍离限制区，球被 A3 获得。

A1 试投；A3 进攻篮板球。

12. A1 试投未中篮，A4 同其他几名队员争抢篮板球时以可控制的方式将球拍给 A5，随即 A5 3 分投中。

A1 试投；A4 进攻篮板球；A5 3 分试投和 3 分投中；A4 助攻。

13. A4 试投未中篮，A5 跳起争抢篮板球，控制球后落到了界线外。

A4 试投；B 队防守球队篮板球。

14. A2 misses a FGA. A3 is fighting for the rebound and in the last moment before falling out of bounds he tips the ball at B4's leg from which the ball goes out of bounds. Team A is rewarded with a throw-in afterwards.

FGA A2; Off Rebound A3.

15. After an unsportsmanlike foul A3 misses the second FTA.

No rebound.

14. A2 试投未中篮。A3 争抢篮板球，在他即将出界时他将球拍到 B4 的腿上，随后球出界。A 队获得掷球入界的球权。

A2 试投；A3 进攻篮板球。

15. 在一起违反体育运动精神的犯规后，A3 第二次罚球尝试未中篮。

不登记篮板球。

第 4 章

FOUR - TURNOVERS

失误

FOUR-TURNOVERS

A turnover is a mistake by an offensive player or team that results in the defensive team gaining possession of the ball, including:

- A bad pass.
- Ball handling or fumbling.
- Any kind of violation or offensive foul.

A turnover can only be committed by the team in control. A team is in control of the ball when:

- A player of that team is holding or dribbling a live ball.
- The ball is at its disposal for a throw-in during an out-of-bounds situation.
- The ball is at the disposal of a player for a free-throw.
- The ball is being passed between team-mates.

If the offensive team is forced into a held-ball by the actions of a defensive player, the result of the alternating possession rule will determine the statistics to be charged:

- If the offensive team gains possession as a result of the alternating possession rule - NO statistics are charged.
- If the defensive team gains possession as a result of the alternating possession rule - charge a turnover to the offensive player at fault and a steal to the defensive player that initiated the turnover.

Turnover types

Ball Handling
An offensive player loses possession while holding or dribbling the ball, or failing to catch a pass that should have been caught.

Violation
A violation by an offensive player or team e.g. travelling, 3 or 5 second violations, backcourt violation, out of bounds, 8 or 24 second violations. 5 second violations during an inbounds play as well as all 8 and 24 second violations are recorded as team turnovers, all other turnovers are recorded as turnovers for a player.

第4章 失误

一次失误是指一名进攻队员或球队发生错误，并导致防守队获得了球权，这些错误包括：

- 一次传球失误。
- 控球或漏接球失误。
- 任何类型的违例或者进攻犯规。

只有控制球队会发生失误。下列情况是球队控制球。

- 该队的某队员正持着或运着一个活球时。
- 在一起界外球情况的掷球入界期间，该队可处理球时。
- 在罚球期间，该队的某队员可处理球时。
- 球在该队队员之间传递时。

如果进攻队由于受迫于防守队的动作而发生一次争球，那么交替拥有规则的判定结果将决定技术统计员如何进行登记：

- 如果依据交替拥有规则应判给进攻队球权，不登记任何数据。
- 如果依据交替拥有规则应判给防守队球权，登记受迫的进攻队员一次失误，并登记致使该失误的防守队员一次抢断。

失误类型

控球失误

进攻队员在持球或运球时失去控制球，或者没有接住本应接住的传球。

违例

一名进攻队员或球队发生违例，例如带球走、3秒或5秒违例、球回后场违例、球出界、8秒或进攻时间违例。其中掷球入界期间的5秒违例以及8秒和进攻时间违例被登记为球队失误，其他失误则被登记为队员的失误。

Offensive Foul
An offensive player commits a foul.

Any Technical, Unsportsmanlike or Disqualifying Foul committed by a player or team in possession are turnovers. If committed by a player on the court they are recorded as a player turnover, otherwise as a team turnover.

Passing
A team loses possession due to a bad pass. The turnover should always be charged to the passer unless the statistician considers that the pass should have been caught, in which case the turnover should be charged to the receiver.

In some situations a turnover could be classified as more than one type, for example when a bad pass causes a team-mate to commit a violation by stepping out of the playing court to catch the ball. The statistician must recognise how the turnover was originally caused. In this example, the bad pass caused the violation, so the player attempting the pass should be charged a turnover (Passing).

There are certain situations where two or more turnovers happen almost instantaneously. The statistician must decide if control of the ball was gained by a team before again losing control. For turnovers, if there is any doubt about whether a player had control of the ball, the statistician should assume that he did not.

Examples

1. A1 has the ball stolen from him by B1 as he is dribbling down the court.

Turnover (Ball Handling) A1, Steal B1.

2. A2 passes the ball and it goes straight out of bounds.

Turnover (Passing) A2.

3. A1 makes a good pass but A4 drops the ball, resulting in B4 picking the ball up.

Turnover (Ball Handling) A4, Steal B4.

4. A2 commits a violation (travelling, double dribble, etc.) that results in the opposition receiving the ball.

Turnover (Violation) A2.

进攻犯规

一名进攻队员发生一起犯规。

任何控制球的队员或球队所发生的技术犯规、违反体育运动精神的犯规或取消比赛资格的犯规都是失误。如果是场上队员发生的犯规，应登记为队员的失误，反之则应登记为球队失误。

传球

球队因传球失误导致失去球权。该失误应登记给传球队员；除非技术统计员认为这是一次应被接住的传球，在这种情况下，该失误则应登记给接传球的队员。

在某些情况下，一次失误可以被登记为不同的类型，例如当一次不到位的传球导致同队队员接球时踩到了界外而发生违例。技术统计员必须认识到这次失误最初是因何而起的。在本例中，是不到位的传球导致了违例，所以传球队员应被登记一次失误（传球失误）。

还有在某些情况下，几乎同时发生了两次或两次以上的失误。技术统计员必须确定在某队再次失去控制球前，该队是否控制过球。在登记失误方面，如果对于一名队员是否控制球存在疑问，那么技术统计员应默认他并未控制过球。

举例

1. A1 在场上运球推进时被 B1 断球。

   A1 失误（控球失误）；B1 抢断。

2. A2 传球，球直接出界了。

   A2 失误（传球失误）。

3. A1 向 A4 传出一次好球，但 A4 丢球，致使 B4 获得了球。

   A4 失误（控球失误）；B4 抢断。

4. A2 发生违例（带球走、两次运球等），致使对方获得了球权。

   A2 失误（违例）。

5. A5 commits a foul whilst his team is on offence (charge, moving screen etc).

Turnover (Offensive Foul) A5.

6. Team A fails to get a shot off and commits a twenty-four second violation.

Turnover (Violation) Team A.

7. A2 picks up the ball after dribbling and is closely guarded by B2. He is unable to shoot or pass the ball and commits a five second violation.

Turnover (Violation) A2.

8. A1 is in possession of the ball when A4 and B4 simultaneously commit double fouls.

As the foul penalties cancel and Team A is awarded the ball out-of-bounds, no turnover exists. Both A4 and B4 are charged with a foul and a foul drawn.

9. A3 is holding the ball when B3 knocks it loose. A3 and B3 dive on the floor and a held-ball situation between the two players occurs. (a) Team A are entitled to the alternating possession. (b) Team B are entitled to the alternating possession.

(a) No statistics are charged.
(b) Turnover (Ball Handling) A3, Steal B3.

10. A2 is called for a technical foul (a) while A3 is dribbling the ball (b) immediately after B5 has stolen the ball from A3.

(a) Technical foul A2; Turnover A2.
(b) Turnover (ballhandling) A3, Steal B5. Technical foul A2. No turnover A2 as his team was not in possession when the technical was called.

11. A4 is trapped in the corner by B5. While trying to save the situation, A4 (a) is called for a travelling violation; (b) throws a pass to A1 which is deflected by B5 and intercepted in the end by B1; (c) throws a pass to A1 which is intercepted by B1 without being touched by B5.

(a) Turnover (travelling) A4.
(b) Turnover (bad pass) A4; Steal B5.
(c) Turnover (bad pass) A4; Steal B1.

5. A5 在 A 队进攻时发生犯规（撞人、移动掩护等）。

A5 失误（进攻犯规）。

6. A 队未能在 24 秒内完成投篮球离手而发生一起违例。

A 队球队失误（违例）。

7. A2 运球结束后持球，并被 B2 严密防守。A2 无法投篮或传球并最终发生了一起 5 秒违例。

A2 失误（违例）。

8. A1 控制球时，A4 和 B4 几乎同时发生了双方犯规。

因为犯规的罚则被抵消，A 队将执行掷球入界，因此没有发生失误。A4 和 B4 应各被登记一次犯规和一次被侵犯。

9. A3 持球时，B3 将球拍掉。A3 和 B3 倒地抢球发生争球。（a）A 队拥有交替拥有的球权；（b）B 队拥有交替拥有的球权。

（a）不登记任何数据；

（b）A3 失误（控球失误），B3 抢断。

10. （a）当 A3 运球时，A2 被判了一次技术犯规。（b）恰好在 B5 从 A3 手中抢断球之后，A2 被判了一次技术犯规。

（a）A2 技术犯规；A2 失误。

（b）A3 失误（控球失误）；B5 抢断；A2 技术犯规。不登记 A2 失误，因为他被判技术犯规时 A 队未控制球。

11. A4 被 B5 严密防守在赛场的角落。在试图摆脱期间，A4（a）被宣判一起带球走违例；（b）将球掷向 A1，球被 B5 接触后最终被 B1 抢断并控制；（c）将球掷向 A1，球被 B1 抢断并控制，其间未被 B5 接触。

（a）A4 失误（带球走）。

（b）A4 失误（传球失误）；B5 抢断。

（c）A4 失误（传球失误）；B1 抢断。

12. A3 is attempting a pass to A5, which is deflected by B3. A5 and B5 are fighting for the loose ball. (a) B5 seems to be in control for a split of a second before stepping out of bounds; (b) B5 seems to be in control for a split of a second before A5 takes the ball away from him; (c) B5 picks up the loose ball, dribbles twice and throws a pass which is intercepted by A4.

(a) We assume there was no change of possession, no statistics are recorded.
(b) We assume there was no change of possession, no statistics are recorded.
(c) Turnover A3 (bad pass); Steal B5; Turnover (bad pass) B5; Steal A4.

13. A1 throws a bad pass to A2. While trying to save the ball, A2 tips the ball to his own backcourt where it is picked up by A3, who is called for a backcourt violation.

Turnover (Bad pass) A1.

12. A3 试图传球给 A5，球被 B3 接触。A5 和 B5 争抢球。（a）B5 看似短暂地控制了球，但 B5 随即踩到了界外；（b）B5 看似短暂地控制了球，但 A5 随即从 B5 手中抢走了球；（c）B5 抢到球，运球两次后传球，但球被 A4 抢断。

（a）我们应假定未发生球权转换，不登记数据。

（b）我们应假定未发生球权转换，不登记数据。

（c）A3 失误（传球失误）；B5 抢断；B5 失误（传球失误）；A4 抢断。

13. A1 向 A2 做出一次低质量的传球。在试图救球时，A2 将球拍回了其本队的后场，球被 A3 获得。裁判员宣判球回后场违例。

A1 失误（传球失误）。

第5章
FIVE - ASSISTS
助攻

FIVE-ASSISTS

An assist is a pass that leads directly to a team-mate scoring.

- A pass to a player inside the paint, who scores from inside the paint is always considered an assist.
- A pass to a player outside the paint, who scores without dribbling is always an assist.
- A pass to a player outside the paint, who scores after one or more dribbles, is considered an assist if the shooter does not need to beat his defender. We don't award an assist if the shooter beats his defender in a 1-on-1 situation who is facing him and is located directly in front of him, between him and the basket. Helpside defenders are not relevant in this sense. An assist is still given in situations when the offensive player is driving by his defender in a 1-on-1 situation if
  - ○ He drives to the basket immediately after receiving the pass AND
  - ○ His defender is caught off-balance

The same principle applies in fast-break situations, with a pass to a player at half-court.

Scoring includes free-throws. If the player who receives the pass is fouled in the act of shooting and makes at least one free-throw, an assist is awarded in the same way as for a FGM.

Additionally the following general rules always apply:

- Only one assist can be given each time a player scores.
- Only the last pass before a shot can be an assist (even if the second to last pass created the play).
- The distance and type of shot and the ease with which a player scores, are not relevant.
- No assist shall be given in a fast-break situation if the player receives the pass in his own half-court before driving to the basket (coast to coast).

第5章　助攻

一次助攻是指一次使自己同队队员直接得分的传球。

- 当球被传给限制区内的一名队员，并由该队员从限制区内得分时，该传球应始终被视为一次助攻。
- 当球被传给限制区外的一名队员，并由该队员未经运球即得分，该传球应始终被视为一次助攻。
- 当球被传给限制区外的一名队员，并由该队员运球一次或多次后得分，且该投篮队员在此期间并无防守压力的话，该传球应被视为一次助攻。如果该投篮队员在一对一情况下被位于他和对方球篮之间的一名防守队员直接/正面防守，则该传球不被视为一次助攻。该情况下，判定助攻与是否出现弱侧协防队员无关。当该进攻队员突破时被其防守队员一对一盯防，如果出现下述情况，仍应登记一次助攻：
  - 进攻队员在接到传球后立即持球突破上篮，并且
  - 其防守队员防守失位。

同样的原则也适用于在快攻中向一名位于中场位置的队员传球时。

得分方式包括罚球。如果接到传球的队员在投篮动作中被犯规，并且至少罚球中篮一次，则如同投中一样登记给传球队员一次助攻。

此外，下述的一般规则也始终适用：

- 一名队员的每次得分只能登记一次助攻。
- 只有投篮前的最后一次传球能记作助攻（即使是倒数第二次传球制造了得分机会）。
- 投篮的距离和方式以及队员得分的难度与助攻没有关系。
- 如果一名队员在自己的半场接到传球后快攻突破上篮（从后场运球至前场上篮），则不应登记助攻。

• No assist is given if the pass is clearly deflected and ends up with a different player than the one it was initially intended for.

Examples

1. After capturing a defensive rebound, A5 makes a full-court pass to A4 who misses a lay-up but has enough time to easily score from the rebound.

No assist, there has been a FGA and offensive rebound between the pass and the score.

2. A5 passes to A4 who hesitates, looks to pass to A3, who is cutting, and then takes and makes the shot.

FGA and FGM A4, Assist A5.

3. A5 passes to A4 who takes one dribble to find balance, and then takes the shot, making it.

Charge an assist to A5, provided A4 was not guarded by a defender facing him.

4. A4 makes a great full-court pass to A5, who only has to hand-off the ball to A3 for an uncontested lay-up that is made.

Even though the pass from A4 created the basket, it was not the last pass before the score. Charge the assist to A5.

5. A3 passes to A5, who is guarded closely by B3, pump fakes, spins, takes one dribble and dunks the ball. He received the pass (a) inside the paint (b) outside the paint.

FGA and FGM A5. (a) Assist A3; (b) no Assist.

6. B1 steals the ball, makes a pass to B2 who is at the centre court line in front of the defence, and then B2 dribbles to the opponents basket for an unopposed lay-up.

Charge B1 with an assist.

7. After a missed shot A2 gets the defensive rebound. He passes the ball to A3 at his own three-point line, who goes coast to coast and scores with an uncontested layup.

- 如果一次传球明显被碰触并最终被另外一名队员（不是原先应当接到传球的队员）接到，则不应登记助攻。

举例

1. 在获得一次防守篮板球后，A5 向 A4 做出全场长传，A4 上篮未中篮但随后有足够的时间抢得篮板球后轻易得分。

没有助攻，在传球和最后得分间发生了一次试投和一次获得进攻篮板球。

2. A5 传球给 A4，A4 迟疑后想寻找机会传球给正在切入的 A3，但随后他选择自己投篮并中篮。

A4 试投和投中；A5 助攻。

3. A5 传球给 A4，A4 通过一次运球来维持平衡，随后 A4 投篮并中篮。

如果 A4 没有被防守队员从正面防守，则登记 A5 一次助攻。

4. A4 向 A5 做出一次绝佳的全场长传，A5 只需手递手传球给 A3 就能使后者完成一次无人防守的上篮。

即使 A4 的传球制造了得分机会，这却不是得分前的最后一次传球。应登记给 A5 一次助攻。

5. A3 传球给正被 B3 严密防守着的 A5，A5 虚晃、转身，紧接着运球一次后扣篮得分。他在接传球时，（a）位于限制区内；（b）位于限制区外。

A5 试投和投中，（a）A3 助攻；（b）没有助攻。

6. B1 断球后传球给位于中线处且面对着防守队员的 B2。B2 随后向对方球篮运球几次后在无人防守的情况下上篮得分。

登记 B1 一次助攻。

7. 在一次投篮未中篮后，A2 获得防守篮板球。他传球给位于本方半场三分线处的 A3。A3 随后在无人防守的情况下从后场运球至前场并上篮得分。

No assist as A3 received the pass in his own half-court.

8.   After a missed shot A2 gets the defensive rebound. He makes a long pass to A3 at half-court in front of the defence. (a) B3 fouls A3 to stop the fast-break and is called for an unsportsmanlike foul. (b) B4 commits a personal (shooting) foul while A3 attempts a layup. In both situations A3 is awarded two free-throws and makes the first and misses the second one.

(a)   Unsportsmanlike Foul B3, Foul Drawn A3, FTA and FTM A3 (no assist).
(b)   Personal Foul B4, Foul Drawn A3, FTA and FTM A3, Assist A2.

9.   A1 inbounds the ball at the baseline underneath his opponents' basket, and passes to A3 who scores a FGM.

Charge A1 with an assist.

10. Immediately following a pass from A2, A3 is fouled in the act of shooting. A3 misses the first free-throw, and makes the second.

Charge A2 with an assist, A3 with two FTA's and one FTM.

没有助攻，因为 A3 是在本方半场接到了传球。

8. 在一次投篮未中篮后，A2 获得防守篮板球。他长传给位于半场且面对着防守队员的 A3。（a）B3 为了阻止快攻而对 A3 犯规，被宣判了一起违反体育运动精神的犯规；（b）B4 在 A3 尝试上篮时对其发生侵人犯规（投篮动作）。在这两种情况下，A3 获得二次罚球，其中第一次罚球中篮，第二次罚球未中篮。

（a）B3 违反体育运动精神的犯规；A3 被侵犯；A3 罚球尝试和罚球得分（无助攻）。

（b）B4 侵人犯规；A3 被侵犯；A3 罚球尝试和罚球得分；A2 助攻。

9. A1 在对方球篮后的端线处掷球入界，该球传给了 A3 并由 A3 完成了投篮并投中。

登记 A1 一次助攻。

10. 在接到 A2 的传球后，A3 立刻做出投篮动作并被犯规。A3 的第一次罚球未中篮，第二次罚球中篮。

登记 A2 一次助攻；登记 A3 进行二次罚球尝试和一次罚球得分。

第6章
SIX - STEALS
抢断

SIX-STEALS

A steal is awarded to a defensive player when his action causes a turnover by an opponent. A steal must always include touching the ball, but does not necessarily have to be controlled.

- Intercepting or deflecting a pass.
- Taking the ball away from an opponent holding or dribbling the ball.
- Picking up a loose ball after a mistake of an offensive player.

No steal is charged if the ball becomes dead and the defensive team is awarded possession of the ball out of bounds - even if the turnover was caused by the action of the defensive player.

The only time a steal can be charged when the ball becomes dead, is when the actions of a defensive player causes a held-ball to occur and his team wins possession as a result of the alternating possession rule.

If a steal is charged to a defensive player, there must be a corresponding turnover charged to an offensive player. (The opposite does not apply – a turnover does not always mean a steal has occurred).

In all situations with more than one defensive player being involved, the player who first deflected the ball and initiated the turnover is charged with the steal.

Examples

1. A5 is dribbling when he mishandles the ball and it bounces toward B4, who recovers it without moving.

Turnover (Ball Handling) A5, Steal B4.

2. A5 is dribbling the ball when B5 knocks it away to B2.

Turnover (Ball Handling) A5, Steal B5.

3. B2 applies hard defensive pressure that causes A2 to commit a violation without B2 touching the ball.

第6章　抢断

当一名防守队员的行为致使一名对方队员发生失误时，应登记该防守队员一次抢断。一次抢断必须包含接触球，但不是一定要控制球。

- 拦截或破坏传球。
- 从一名持球或运球的对方队员手中抢得球。
- 在一名进攻队员出现错误后控制了其脱手的球。

如果球成死球且防守队获得掷球入界球权，则不登记抢断——即使这次失误是防守队员的行为引起的。

唯一一种在球成死球时登记抢断的情况是：当防守队员的行为致使场上发生争球，且交替拥有的结果是该队员的球队获得了球权。

如果登记给一名防守队员一次抢断，就一定会有一名进攻队员被登记对应的失误。（反之，则不成立——一次失误不总是由于一次抢断造成）

在所有多于一名防守队员参与的情况下，应登记给首先破坏球或者最初造成对方失误的队员一次抢断。

举例

1. A5 运球时失误，球反弹至 B4 处，B4 站在原地便获得了控制球。

A5 失误（控球失误）；B4 抢断。

2. A5 运球时被 B5 将球拍走，B2 获得球。

A5 失误（控球失误）；B5 抢断。

3. B2 对 A2 施加防守压力并迫使 A2 违例，但 B2 没有接触过球。

Turnover (Violation) A2 but no steal.

4. B5 deflects a pass from A4 intended for A5 who, in a reflex action, tries to catch the ball, but can only deflect it over the sideline. Team B is awarded the right to a throw in from the sideline.

Turnover (Passing) A4 but no steal.

5. B5 deflects a pass from A4, intended for A5, into the open court where A5 and B2 both grab the ball and a held-ball is called. Team B is awarded the ball for a throw in from the sideline (alternating possession rule).

Turnover (Passing) A4, Steal B5. A5 and B2 receive no statistics.

6. A2 passes the ball directly out of bounds.

No steal is charged, whilst A2 is charged with a turnover (Passing).

7. A1 is dribbling the ball and unintentionally dribbles the ball off his foot. The ball rolls along the playing court and is picked up by B2.

Turnover (Ball Handling) A1, Steal B2.

8. Team A gain possession of the ball following the opening jump ball.

No steal is charged as no team was in possession of the ball before the jump ball.

9. A4 misses a FGA. The ball hits the rim, bounces off the floor and is caught by B2.

No steal is charged. Charge A4 with an FGA and B2 with a defensive rebound.

10. A1 is driving to the basket. Help-side defender B2 anticipates this play and provokes an offensive foul being called against A1.

Turnover (offensive foul) A1. No steal is recorded.

A2 失误（违例），但没有抢断。

4. B5 破坏了 A4 传向 A5 的球，A5 做出反应并试图去拿球，但最终将球拍出了边线。B 队获得了位于边线外掷球入界的权利。

A4 失误（传球失误）；没有抢断。

5. B5 破坏了 A4 传向 A5 的球，随后球在赛场的开阔区域被 A5 和 B2 同时抓住，裁判员宣判争球。B 队获得了位于边线外掷球入界的权利（依据交替拥有规则）。

A4 失误（传球失误）；B5 抢断。不登记 A5 和 B2 任何数据。

6. A2 直接将球传出界线。

不登记抢断，但登记 A2 一次失误（传球失误）。

7. A1 运球期间意外地将球运到了他脚上。球随后在赛场上滚动并被 B2 控制。

A1 失误（控球失误）；B2 抢断。

8. A 队在开场跳球后获得控制球。

不登记抢断，因为任一球队都未在跳球前拥有过球权。

9. A4 试投未中篮，球接触篮圈后落地反弹，并被 B2 拿到。

不登记抢断。登记 A4 一次试投和 B2 一次防守篮板球。

10. A1 持球向球篮突破。协防队员 B2 作出预判并造成了 A1 进攻犯规。

A1 失误（进攻犯规）；不登记抢断。

第7章
SEVEN - BLOCKED SHOTS
封盖

SEVEN-BLOCKED SHOTS

A blocked shot is awarded to a player any time he appreciably makes contact with the ball to alter the flight of a FGA and the shot is missed. It recognises a clear rejection or deflection of a shot by a defensive player. The ball may or may not have left the hand of the shooter for the block to be counted.

The act of shooting, for statistical purposes, shall be an upward and/or forward motion toward the basket with the intention of trying for a goal.

In situations where the ball is knocked loose before it is in flight:
• In case the ball was above shoulder height a FGA, Blocked Shot and Rebound are recorded.
• In case the ball was below shoulder height, a Turnover and Steal are recorded if the defensive team gains possession; if in the same situation the offensive team stays in possession, then no statistics are recorded.

Like for any other missed FGA, a rebound must follow a blocked shot unless immediately following the blocked shot, the period ends or a twenty four second violation occurs.

Examples

1. A5 shoots and the ball is touched by B5 in an attempt to block the shot. The ball continues into the basket.

Since the ball continued into the basket, B5's touching it did not alter its flight appreciably. Ignore the touching, charge A5 with a FGA and a FGM, but do not charge B5 with a blocked shot.

2. A5 before going for a dunk attempt has the ball stripped at waist-height by B5, before it leaves A5's hands. The ball is recovered by B4.

Turnover (Ball Handling) A5,Steal B5.

3. A5 is driving through the restricted area and has the ball stripped by B5. The ball ends up with B4.

Turnover (Ball handling) A5, Steal B5.

第7章 封盖

当一名队员在一次对方球员试投中明显地接触了球且改变了球的飞行线路，并最终使投篮未中时，应登记该队员一次封盖。封盖意味着一名防守队员对一次投篮的拦截或破坏。一次封盖既可能发生在球离开投篮队员的手之前，也可能发生在球离开投篮队员的手之后。

对于数据统计而言，为了得分而将球朝向对方球篮向上和 / 或向前移动时，是一次投篮动作。

在所有球尚未离手即被拍掉的情况下：

- 如果球在队员肩部以上，则登记一次试投、封盖和篮板球。
- 如果球在队员肩部以下，且如果防守队员获得了球权，则登记一次失误和抢断；相同情况下如果进攻队依然控制球，则不登记任何数据。

在任何其他未中篮的试投中，一次封盖之后一定紧随着一次篮板球，除非在封盖后该节比赛结束或发生进攻时间违例。

举例

1. A5 投篮，B5 尝试封盖并接触球。球最终进入球篮。

球最终进入了球篮，所以 B5 对球的接触并未明显地改变球的飞行轨迹。应忽略这次接触，登记 A5 一次试投和投中，但不登记 B5 封盖。

2. A5 扣篮尝试，即将离手的球被 B5 在齐腰位置的高度打掉。随后球被 B4 控制。

A5 失误（控球失误）；B5 抢断。

3. A5 在限制区运球突破时被 B5 将球打掉。随后 B4 控制球。

A5 失误（控球失误）；B5 抢断。

4. A2 shoots a FGA which (a) is blocked by B4 whilst the ball is in upward motion, the ball going out of bounds (b) is blocked by B4 whilst the ball is on its way down towards the basket and is called as a defensive goaltending violation by the referees.

(a) FGA A2, Blocked Shot B4, Offensive team rebound Team A.

(b) FGA and FGM A2.

5. A3 shoots a three-point jump shot which is blocked by B4. A3 catches the ball immediately and shoots another three-point jump shot which goes in.

3FGA A3, Blocked Shot B4, Offensive Rebound A3, 3FGA and 3FGM A3.

6. A2 attempts a three-point jump shot. The ball bounces off the rim and B1 prevents it from going in by tipping it away. A3 picks up the loose ball.

3FGA A2, Offensive Rebound A3. Note: a Blocked Shot can't be recorded after the ball has hit the rim.

7. A1 is driving to the basket and is fouled by B1 in the act of shooting. He manages to release the shot, which is blocked by help-side defender B2 (the shot would have counted if made).

Personal Foul B1, Foul Drawn A1. No other statistics apply in this situation (as the shooter is fouled, no FGA is recorded – and without a FGA there can't be a Blocked Shot).

4. A2 试投，（a）球在向上飞行时被 B4 封盖，球出界；（b）球在飞向球篮且向下飞行时被 B4 接触，裁判员宣判一起防守干涉得分。

（a）A2 试投；B4 封盖；A 队进攻球队篮板球。

（b）A2 试投和投中。

5. A3 尝试 3 分跳投，被 B4 封盖。A3 随即拿到球并再次尝试 3 分跳投，球中篮。

A3 的 3 分试投；B4 封盖；A3 进攻篮板球；A3 进行 3 分试投和 3 分投中。

6. A2 尝试 3 分跳投。球从篮圈上弹起，B1 为防止球进入球篮而将球拍走。A3 控制了球。

A2 的 3 分试投；A3 进攻篮板球。注意：球接触篮圈后，就不能再登记一次封盖。

7. A1 持球向球篮突破，随后在做投篮动作时被 B1 犯规。A1 最终投篮球离手，但球被协防队员 B2 封盖（否则如果球中篮，应计得分）。

B1 侵人犯规；A1 被侵犯。此情况下不再登记其他数据（因为投篮队员被犯规，所以不登记试投；又因为不登记试投，就不应登记封盖）。

第 8 章
EIGHT - FOULS
犯规

EIGHT-FOULS

A foul is called on a player following a decision by a referee. Personal, technical, unsportsmanlike and disqualifying fouls can be called on a player. Technical and disqualifying fouls can be called on a coach or team bench personnel. It is important to differentiate between the types of fouls, should the statistics software allow this. Technical and disqualifying fouls called on the coach or team bench personnel are recorded against the coach and are not counted as team fouls.

In case the software allows to distinguish between "shooting" and "non-shooting" fouls, a shooting foul is any foul called by the officials as a foul "in the act of shooting". A foul resulting in FTs only because of team fouls is a non-shooting foul.

Fouls Drawn

Any time a player is fouled, a foul drawn is charged to that player. In the case of a disqualifying foul, if the foul is physically committed on a player, then a foul drawn is charged to the player who has been fouled.

Examples

1. A3 is dribbling the ball and commits a charge on B2.

Turnover (Offensive Foul) A3, Personal Foul A3, Foul Drawn B2 (no steal for B2).

2. A2 is holding the ball when he is fouled by B2.

Foul drawn A2, Personal Foul B2.

3. A1 commits a disqualifying foul by (a) insulting the referee (b) hitting B2 with his elbow

(a) Disqualifying Foul A1, Turnover A1.
(b) Disqualifying Foul A1, Turnover A1, Foul Drawn B2.

第8章 犯规

宣判队员犯规是裁判员经判定后作出的决定。一名队员可能被宣判侵人的、技术的、违反体育运动精神的和取消比赛资格的犯规。一名教练员或球队席人员可能被宣判技术的和取消比赛资格的犯规。区分犯规的类型十分重要，数据统计软件应能实现：将教练员或球队席人员的技术犯规和取消比赛资格的犯规登记给教练员，但不计入全队犯规。

如果使用的软件允许区分"投篮"和"非投篮"犯规，那么一次投篮犯规指的是裁判员在"投篮动作"期间宣判的任一犯规。如果判给罚球的原因仅仅是全队犯规，则该犯规是非投篮犯规。

被侵犯

每当一名队员被其他队员犯规，他应被登记一次被侵犯。在一起取消比赛资格的犯规中，如果该犯规包含对一名队员的身体接触，则被犯规的队员应被登记一次被侵犯。

举例

1. A3 运球时对 B2 发生撞人犯规。

A3 失误（进攻犯规）；A3 侵人犯规；B2 被侵犯（不登记 B2 抢断）。

2. A2 持球时被 B2 犯规。

A2 被侵犯；B2 侵人犯规。

3. A1 被判一起取消比赛资格的犯规，因为他（a）辱骂裁判员；（b）肘击 B2。

（a）A1 取消比赛资格的犯规；A1 失误。

（b）A1 取消比赛资格的犯规；A1 失误；B2 被侵犯。

附录 A
Annex A - Types of shots
投篮类型

Annex A-Types of shots

In case the software requires the type of shot being entered, the following types or a subset thereof shall be available:

Jump shot
A shot taken by jumping up in the air and usually releasing the basketball at the peak of the jump. It is used most frequently for mid- to long-range shots, including three-point attempts.

Layup
A close-range shot usually involves the shooter banking the basketball off the backboard, but can also be over the front of the rim. It is commonly a one-handed shot made by holding the ball from below and releasing it using an upwards motion of the arm as close to the basket as possible. A layup can also be a quick shot where the offensive player catches the ball next to the basket.

Driving layup
A close-range shot following a dribble drive to the basket either when the defence is back and set, or on a fast break. The shot is usually banked off the backboard but can also be over the front of the rim.

Dunk
A dunk is a play in which a player brings the ball above the rim and slams it down into the hoop with one or two hands in which the player's hand(s) hit the top of the rim.

Putback dunk
When a player on the offensive team grabs an offensive rebound and then immediately slams the basketball forcefully through the hoop, with one or two hands in which the player's hand(s) hit the top of the rim.

附录 A　投篮类型

如果软件要求输入投篮的类型，应列入以下投篮类型或它们的集合：

跳投

跳投指的是队员跳起至空中并通常在最高点时球离手的投篮。跳投在中距离和远距离投篮中最常见，也包括 3 分试投。

上篮

上篮是一种近距离的投篮，通常由投篮队员使球经篮板反弹而完成，但上篮也可能直接从篮圈正面的上空完成。上篮一般都是由单手完成的投篮动作，队员通常通过持球并使手臂在离球篮尽可能近的距离做出自下而上的球离手动作来完成上篮。上篮同样可能是进攻队员在靠近篮下处拿球后迅速做出的投篮。

运球上篮

无论防守队员是否就位，又或者是否在一次快攻中，在运球突破后所做出的近距离投篮是一次运球上篮。运球上篮通常通过球经篮板反弹而完成，但也可能直接从篮圈正面的上空完成。

扣篮

扣篮指的是一名队员以单手或双手接触篮圈并同时将球从篮圈上方用力扣入篮圈的得分方式。

补扣

补扣指的是进攻队的一名队员在获得一次进攻篮板球后立即以单手或双手接触篮圈并同时将球用力扣入篮圈的得分方式。

Putback tip-in

When a player on the offensive team grabs an offensive rebound and then immediately scores a field goal next to the basket. This often can have the offensive player jumping up and tipping the ball into the basket with one hand without coming back down onto the floor.

Alley-oop

A shot involving a player catching a pass in the air and finishing with a layup or dunk before landing back on the court.

Hook shot

A one-handed shot involving the player with the basketball turning side on to the basket with the shooting hand farthest from the basket, and then extending their shooting arm and flicking the basketball over their head in a circular motion towards the basket.

Floating jump shot

The basketball is shot off one foot without stopping often like a driving layup but further away from the basket. It can be shot off the run, off the dribble, or off of a catch and it can be banked in or swished and often has a high arc to keep from being blocked.

Fadeaway jump shot

When the shot is taken while the player is jumping away from the basket. This shot is used to create space between the shooter and their defender and can be done from anywhere on the court and can be done jumping straight back or to the side.

Turnaround jump shot

When the player receives the ball with their back to the basket, then starts their shot facing away from the basket and then turns mid-air while jumping to shoot. They may turn all the way to face the basket but sometimes they only turn part way around and shoot while facing side on to the basket.

Step back jump shot

The player usually fakes a drive to the basket then stops and takes a step back to create space between them and the defender before shooting.

补篮

补篮指的是进攻队的一名队员在获得一次进攻篮板球后立即在靠近篮下处中篮得分。进攻队员经常会以跳起到空中并通过单手拍击球进篮的方式完成一次补篮，而非落回赛场地面后再进行补篮。

空中接力

空中接力指的是一名队员在空中接球，并在落回赛场地面之前所完成的一次上篮或扣篮。

勾手投篮

勾手投篮指的是一名持球队员侧对球篮并用离球篮较远的那只手做出的投篮，该投篮通过在投篮队员头部上方延伸手臂，朝向球篮做出弧形动作，并让球从手中拨离的方式完成。

抛投

抛投指的是在不停顿运动的过程中，在距离球篮较远的位置单脚跳起做出的类似上篮的投篮。这样的投篮，球离手可能发生在跑动中、运球期间或接球时，并通过打板或空心中篮方式得分。抛投的抛物线往往很高，为的是避免被封盖。

后仰跳投

后仰跳投指的是一名队员向非球篮方向跳起并做出的投篮。做出这样的投篮为的是在投篮队员和其防守队员之间制造空间。后仰跳投可以在赛场上的任何地点做出，并且投篮队可以向后方或侧方跳起。

转身跳投

转身跳投指的是一名队员接球时背对球篮，随后在身体并未正对球篮时跳起，并在半空中转身投篮。他们可能完成了转身并使身体完全正对球篮，但有些时候，他们未完成转身并在身体依然侧对球篮时做出投篮。

后撤步跳投

队员通常会做出准备持球突破上篮的假动作，然后停步并向后迈出一步以在他们和其防守队员之间制造空间，并做出投篮。

Pullup jump shot

The shooter stops quickly off the dribble and pulls up to shoot a jump shot while the defender(s) are usually still in a low position defending the drive.

急停跳投

急停跳投指的是投篮队员迅速停止运球后起跳并做出的投篮。急停跳投期间，防守队员通常还处于降低重心防守突破时的状态。

附录 B
Annex B - Types of turnovers
失误类型

Annex B-Types of turnovers

The following list defines possible values for the types of turnovers:

- Bad pass
- Ball handling / fumbling
- Out of bounds
- Travelling
- 3 seconds
- 5 seconds
- 8 seconds
- 24 seconds
- Backcourt violation
- Offensive Foul
- Technical / disqualifying foul by team in possession
- Offensive goaltending
- Double dribble
- Carrying / palming
- Other

附录 B 失误类型

以下列出了可能的失误类型：

- 传球失误

- 控球失误 / 漏接失误

- 出界

- 带球走

- 3 秒违例

- 5 秒违例

- 8 秒违例

- 进攻时间违例

- 球回后场违例

- 进攻犯规

- 控制球队的技术犯规 / 取消比赛资格的犯规

- 进攻干涉得分

- 两次运球

- 携带球 / 翻腕

- 其他

附录 C
Annex C - Additional data
附加数据

Annex C-Additional data

In this annex, some additional data is defined which is typically calculated by the software and therefore not directly relevant for the work of a statistician.

Time / minutes played

All substitutions are entered in the software and for each player, the playing time is calculated accordingly. In case minutes played are only shown in minutes (i.e. without seconds) the following rounding shall be applied:

- Minutes with less than 30 seconds shall be rounded down.
- Minutes with 30 seconds or more shall be rounded up.
- 0 minutes will be rounded up to 1 minute, regardless of the value of seconds.
- Any value with 1 minute less than the maximum time (e.g. 39 minutes for a game played 4x10 minutes) will be rounded down for any value of seconds to indicate the player did not play the entire game.
- A player who did not enter the court is indicated with "DNP" (did not play) instead of a value for minutes and seconds.

For statistical purposes, a game with DNP does not count as a game played for the player.

Points In The Paint
The total number of points scored by a team from a FGM that originates inside the restricted area. This includes all jump shots, hook shots, lay-ups, dunks etc.

Points Off Turnovers
The total number of points scored by a team during the possession following an opponent turnover. This is the case regardless of the type of turnover, whether the ball goes out of bounds, and the points can come from a FGM or FTM(s).

This does not apply to a FGM or FTM in an additional possession, following a foul being called on a player of the defensive team after a FGA or FGM.

附录 C　附加数据

在此附录中，有些附加数据是数据统计软件直接计算而得出的，因此它们和技术统计员的工作没有直接关系。

上场时间 / 分钟

数据统计软件会记录所有的替换，并能对应计算出每名队员的上场时间。如果上场时间只能以分钟显示（比如，无法显示秒数），应运用下列原则计算：

- 少于 30 秒的时间不作为 1 分钟被登记。
- 多于或等于 30 秒的时间作为 1 分钟被登记。
- 不管上场多少秒，如果分钟数是 0，应作为 1 分钟被登记。
- 在上场时间与全场时间相差不足 1 分钟的情况下（比如在 4×10 分钟的比赛中上场 39 分钟），其秒数应被忽略以表示他没有打满全场。
- 比赛中未上场的队员应被标记"DNP"（未比赛），而不是分钟和秒数值。

对于数据统计而言，如果一名队员在一场比赛中被标记"DNP"，就视其未参加过这场比赛。

限制区得分

某队在限制区内投中得分的总和。这包括所有的跳投、勾手投篮、上篮、扣篮等。

在对方失误后得分

某队在对方失误后获得球权，并随后得分的总和。此处不考虑失误的类型，无论失误后球是否出界，并且，得分可以源自投篮也可以源自罚球。

如果在一次试投或投中后宣判了一起防守队中某名队员的犯规，且罚则是一次额外的球权，则本规定不适用。

Second Chance Points

The total number of points scored by a team following an offensive rebound and before their opponents regain possession. This is the case regardless of whether the ball goes out of bounds, and the points can come from a FGM or FTM(s).

This does not apply to a FGM or FTM in an additional possession, following a foul being called on a player of the defensive team after a FGA or FGM.

Bench Points
The total number of points scored by a team excluding the starting five players.

Score Tied
The number of times the score was tied during the game (excludes 0-0).

Lead Changed
The number of times the lead changed from one team to the other during the game.

Largest Lead
The largest lead each team had during the game, and when this occurred (period and time).

Largest Scoring Run
The largest margin of consecutive points scored by a team without any points being scored by their opponent.

二次进攻得分

在某队获得进攻篮板球后并且在对手获得控制球前所完成的得分的总和。此处不考虑球是否出界，并且得分可以源自投篮也可以源自罚球。

该得分的登记不适用于：在一次试投或投中之后，防守队的一名队员被宣判了一次犯规，并在犯规所带来的球权中再次出现一次试投或投中。

替补队员得分

某队除首发 5 名队员之外的其他队员得分的总和。

得分相等

比赛过程中两队得分相等的次数（除 0：0 之外）。

领先队变化

比赛过程中从某队领先变为另一队领先的次数。

最大分差

每队在比赛中领先的最大分差，以及该分差是何时发生的（节和时间点）。

最大连续得分区间

在某队未得分期间被另一队连续得分的最大区间。

NOTE:

NOTE:

NOTE:

NOTE:

NOTE:

NOTE:

NOTE:

NOTE:

NOTE:

NOTE:

NOTE:

NOTE:

策划编辑：曾　莉
责任编辑：曾　莉　张志富
责任校对：王泓滢
版式设计：李　鹤

图书在版编目（CIP）数据

篮球技术统计员手册 / 中国篮球协会审定. —— 北京：
北京体育大学出版社，2023.7
　　ISBN 978-7-5644-3847-0

　　Ⅰ.①篮… Ⅱ.①中… Ⅲ.①篮球运动 – 运动技术 –
体育统计 – 手册 Ⅳ.①G841.19-62

中国国家版本馆CIP数据核字(2023)第112055号

篮球技术统计员手册
LANQIU JISHU TONGJIYUAN SHOUCE

中国篮球协会　审定

出版发行：	北京体育大学出版社
地　　址：	北京市海淀区农大南路1号院2号楼2层办公B-212
邮　　编：	100084
网　　址：	http://cbs.bsu.edu.cn
发 行 部：	010-62989320
邮 购 部：	北京体育大学出版社读者服务部 010-62989432
印　　刷：	河北盛世彩捷印刷有限公司
开　　本：	880mm×1230mm　　　1/32
成品尺寸：	145mm×210mm
印　　张：	3
字　　数：	80千字
版　　次：	2023年7月第1版
印　　次：	2023年7月第1次印刷
定　　价：	27.00元